Life at the SEASHORE

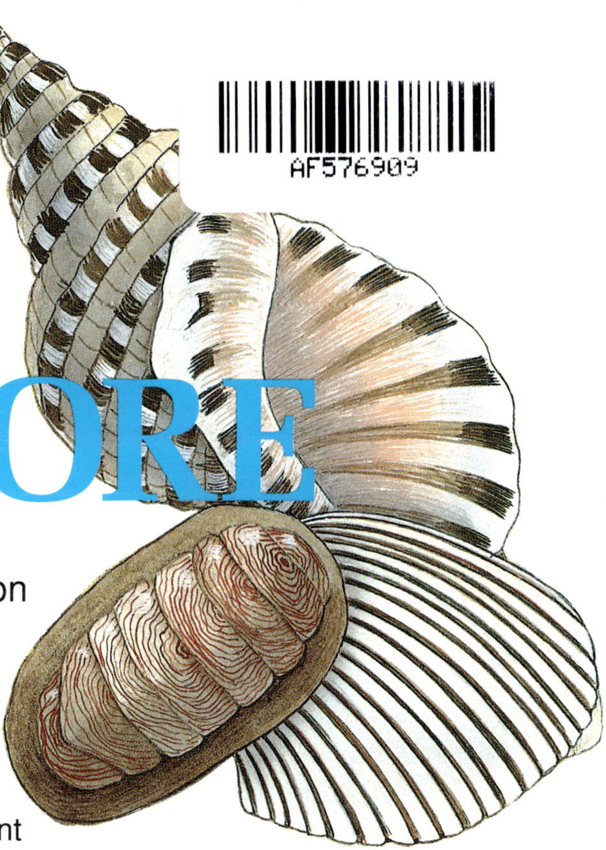

Written by Helen Mason

Illustrated by Martin J. Magee

Editor
Catherine Hunt

Art Director
Maggie Clough

Durkin Hayes Publishing Ltd.
3312 Mainway, Burlington, Ontario L7M 1A7
One Colomba Drive, Niagara Falls, New York 14305

What is Special about a Seashore?

Lick your lips as you walk beside the seashore. What do you taste?

The ocean contains saltwater. Because of the wind and the spray from the waves, everything along a seashore — including you — is covered with small particles of salt.

Can you take the salt out of saltwater?

TRY THIS EXPERIMENT TO FIND OUT.

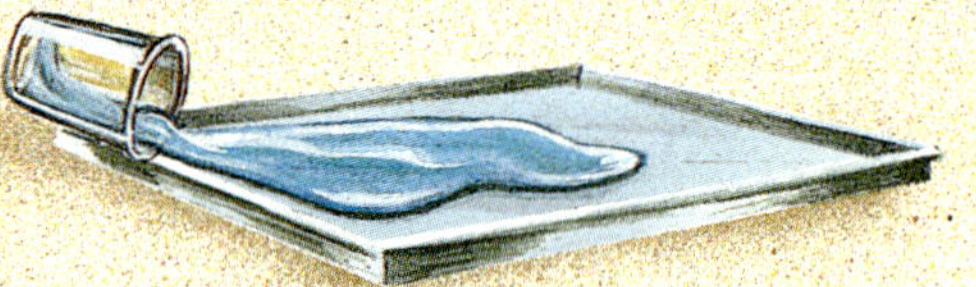

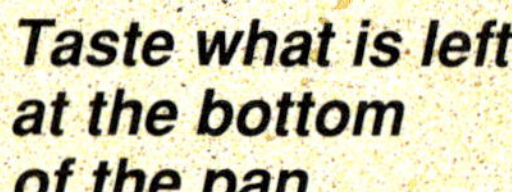

Taste what is left at the bottom of the pan.

1. Collect saltwater from a clean area. 2. Pour the water into a flat pan.
3. Leave the pan in a place where a warm wind blows across it. 4. Let the water evaporate.

Sea salt and table salt are not quite the same. Sea salt contains table salt plus other salts and minerals.

THE CHANGING SEASHORE

Something else makes the seashore special. Watch the level of water on the beach during the day. What do you notice?

Along most shorelines the level of the water rises and falls twice a day. This movement of water is called a tide.

At high tide, water covers most of the seashore, filling in the spaces between the rocks. At low tide the seashore is uncovered. When the water goes down, it leaves a line of shells, seaweed, driftwood, and other things that float.

How many different items can you find here?

Sandy Shores

Beach sand is made up of tiny rocks and pieces of shells. The pounding waves have ground them down over many years.

MAKE A SAND COLLECTION

Collect sand from different places at the beach. Get some from the edge of the water, at the top of a sand dune, and from the center of the beach. Now look closely.

What is the same about your samples?

What is different?

How many different colors and shapes can you see?

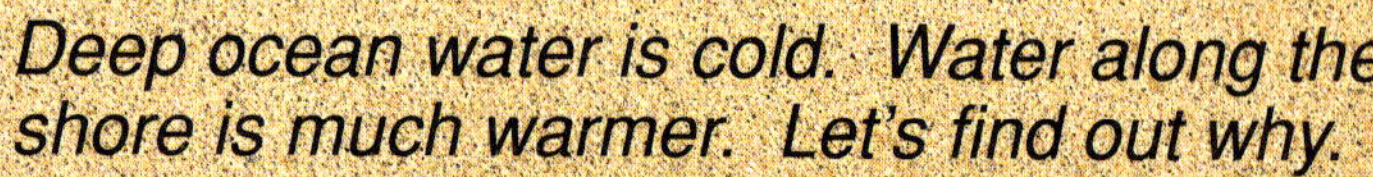

Deep ocean water is cold. Water along the shore is much warmer. Let's find out why.

Place a pieplate filled with sand in the hot sun. Leave it for several hours. Fill a glass with cold water and take its temperature. Pour the cold water over the hot sand. Now take the temperature. What happens to the temperature? Why do you think water at the seashore is warmer?

PUT YOUR NAME IN SAND

Beachcombers are people who love to wander along the beach, collecting treasures they find. Many beachcombers like to write their names in the sand. Waves and animals leave their marks on the sand too. The beach is always changing with the wind and waves.

What signatures can you find here?

Rocky Shores

Some seashores are covered with rock. Waves crashing against the rocks gradually wear them smooth. The sea also makes interesting rock carvings. Tunnels, caves and channels are often created by the waves. New Zealand's Piercey Island and Canada's Percé Rock have a similar name. How do you think they earned it?

(Hint: percé is the French word for pierced.)

At high tide water flows over the rocks at the shore. At low tide some of the water is left behind, creating a tidal pool. The tidal pool is teeming with life. Look for animals that cling to the rocks. What animals can you find?

When the rocks are covered with water, the **limpet** moves slowly on the rocks, eating seaweed. When the tide goes out, it clamps itself down hard so that it cannot be moved.

A sea anemone looks like a beautiful flower. When another animal comes near, the anemone's tentacles close around it. The poison in the tentacles kills the prey.

Clown fish are unique. They live protected among the tentacles. This tricks other animals into believing it is a safe place.

The serpent star has long, wavy arms. It can move up, down and sideways.

A sea urchin is covered with sharp spines that help it move. It feeds on plants that grow on the rocks.

MAKE A SEA MONSTER

Collect some nicely shaped stones to create a sea monster. Glue them together. You may want to add pipecleaners for horns and beads or buttons for eyes. What about toothpick claws? Will you paint your monster?

Exploring the Harbor

A harbor is a sheltered place on the shore where it is deep enough for boats to land safely. How many different boats call this harbor home?

MAKE YOUR OWN FISHING BOAT

All you will need is one small, flat piece of wood and some smaller square pieces. Ask an adult to help you cut a point in one end of the flat piece of wood. Nail on the square pieces to make the ship's cabin. If you have some round spools or other interesting pieces of wood, you might like to add a pulley for bringing in the anchor. Use an old necklace or key chain as an anchor chain. A mesh onion bag will make a good fish net. Will this boat have fishing lines? How can you make them?

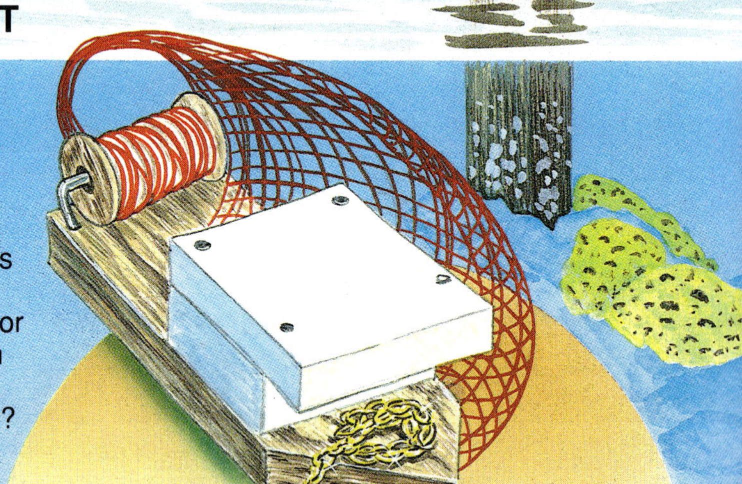

OUTSMART THE TIDE

Have a guessing game with the tide. When the tide is coming in, make a mark on the dock pier where you think the water will be in the next hour. Were you right? Try the same game over several days. Do you get better?

EXPLORE THE DOCKS

Take a close look at and around the docks. How many different plants and animals can you find living there?

Barnacles use a very strong glue they make inside their bodies to stick themselves to just about any surface under the water. They gather on ships, docks, rocks, whales, shellfish, turtles, even floating garbage! The rock barnacle spends its life upside down — could you?

Sponges are plant-like animals that attach themselves to rocks and shells in shallow parts of the sea. The water flowing through the holes in the sponge carries food and oxygen.

Watch a fishing boat come into the harbor. What is following in the air? A noisy crowd of gulls is swooping and gliding around the boat, hoping for some unwanted fish or food scraps.

Saltwater and freshwater meet in a special place at the seashore. We call this a salt marsh.

A salt marsh forms when water from a stream or river flows to the seashore and mixes with saltwater. The beach protects the salt marsh from the force of ocean storms. At high tide seawater covers the marsh. It leaves a wet, muddy bottom at low tide.

Grass is important to the salt marsh. The plants slow down the ocean currents. They also trap the soil. When the grass dies, its stems cover the marsh and prevent it from drying out.

In this protected area other plants and animals can make the marsh their home. What animals can you see here using the grass for their homes and food?

The Salt Marsh

HAVE A BOAT RACE

Measure ten paces along a marshy stream where no grass is growing. Time how long it takes your wooden boat or a leaf to travel that distance. Mark the same distance in an area where grass is blocking part of the stream. How long does it take your boat to travel that section of stream? Can you explain the difference?

HOW SALTY IS THE SALT MARSH?

Find out by collecting equal quantities of water from different parts of the marsh. Make a note of where you collect each sample. Then pour the samples into separate flat pans. Let the water evaporate. **Which sample has the most salt? Which has the least? Do you know why?** (Hint: Think again about where you collected each sample.)

Brrrr.....COLD!

The Arctic and Antarctic have the coldest seashores in the world. They are covered with ice for most of the year.

There are two types of ice in the polar regions: pack ice and icebergs. Pack ice is formed from seawater and is only one or two years old. Icebergs are made from freshwater glaciers formed over thousands of years. In the spring and summer the pack ice begins to melt. As the ice sheets move, icebergs are often split or "calved," and they begin to travel in the direction of the equator. Antarctic icebergs over 20 km long have been seen!

Some animals have special ways that help them live on icy seashores. Penguins can't fly. But they can slide almost as fast as a person running. How might this help them in their Antarctic home?

Penguins are white on one side and black on the other. They turn one way if they want to get warmer. They turn the other way if they want to cool off. Which way is which? You can check by placing two thermometers in a sunny location. Cover one with a sheet of black construction paper. Cover the other with white construction paper. Does the color make a difference to the temperature reading on the thermometer?

Did you know that normal seawater has ten times as much salt as frozen seawater? As the water freezes the salt (brine) leaves the ice. In the summer people can drink the water from the surface of the sea ice!

The **Arctic tern** loves cold weather. While most birds move from a cold to a warm place for the winter, the Arctic tern migrates from the South to the North Pole. That's a round trip of 40,000 km or 25,000 miles.

MAKE YOUR OWN ICEBERG

Put an ice cube in a glass of water. How much of the ice cube is above the surface of the water? How much is below? You can see why ship captains steer away from icebergs. They never know how much might be hidden beneath the surface.

Which icebergs last the longest? Experiment by freezing different amounts of water. Place them all in the same pail of water. Which one lasts the longest? What happens to the temperature of the water around the ice as it melts?

Sea mammals like the **seal** and the **walrus** have a thick layer of fat, muscle and fur to keep them warm. The **polar bear** is the largest land predator in the Arctic; it weighs about 2000 kg. An excellent swimmer, it uses its forepaws as paddles and its back paws as a rudder.

Plant Me by the Sea

When we think of seashores, we usually think of sand and boats, but seashore plants are important too. Above the beach tall plants trap the sand blown by the wind on the sand dunes. Only hardy plants can grow here in the heat and salt spray from the ocean.

Hiding in the tangled roots of eelgrass are tiny plants and animals. Green skeleton shrimp cling to the leaves. They are waiting for their dinner to swim by. But skeleton shrimp are the favorite meal of stalked jellyfish. Stalked jellyfish can't swim. They too attach themselves to eelgrass.

HOW IS GRASS IMPORTANT TO ALLIGATORS?

Sawgrass is at the beginning of an important food chain in a warm salt marsh. As the sawgrass dies, it forms a mat on the surface of the water. This mat is home for many tiny plants and animals. These are eaten by mosquitoes which in turn are eaten by tadpoles and salamanders. Small fish, frogs, turtles and minnows eat the tadpoles and salamanders. They are eaten by larger wading birds, raccoons, otters, snakes — and alligators.

Some animals depend on alligators for a good home. Alligators live in deep holes that they dig with their claws and tail. During dry weather, frogs, fish, crayfish and mosquitoes can live in these holes.

MAKE A PLANKTON NET

Sometimes you can see plankton that looks like a slimy green mass on the surface of the ocean. Try collecting some by sewing or stapling a piece of material to a bent wire coat hanger. Pull your net through the water. Use a magnifying glass to look at the small green plants and animals inside. The plankton is food for many creatures.

Plants can depend on animals too. Sometimes seaweed roots will begin to grow around a shellfish clinging to a rock at the bottom. When the shellfish dies, the plant is no longer anchored and the seaweed dies.

Learning to Live with THE SEA

Are you hungry and tired after a day at the seashore? Do you wish that you had spare arms for carrying all your treasures? What about a pouch for extra food? And a special machine that could change saltwater into chocolate milkshakes?

Many seashore animals have developed special body parts and ways of living that help them live more easily. These are called adaptations. Here are some of them.

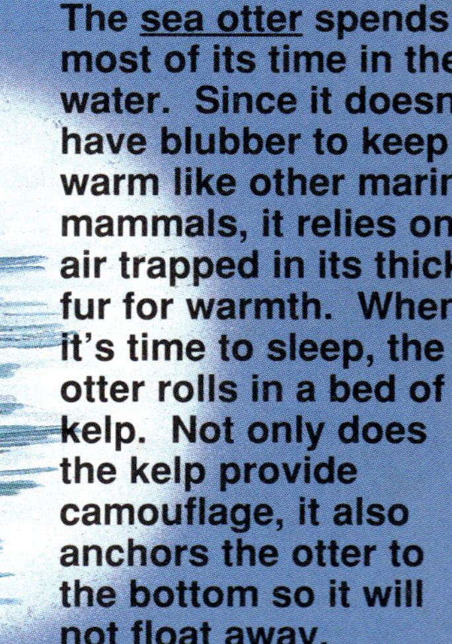

Puffins swim underwater to catch fish. When their mouths open to catch one fish, a special elastic lip stops others from falling out.

There isn't a lot of food in the Arctic where the polar bear lives. That's why the polar bear must have very keen senses. It can see across about 2 km or 1.25 miles. It can smell seal meat 30 km or 19 miles away.

The sea otter spends most of its time in the water. Since it doesn't have blubber to keep it warm like other marine mammals, it relies on air trapped in its thick fur for warmth. When it's time to sleep, the otter rolls in a bed of kelp. Not only does the kelp provide camouflage, it also anchors the otter to the bottom so it will not float away.

<u>Seals</u> in the Antarctic spend the winter under about 2 meters (6 feet) of pack ice. How do you think they breathe? They must spend several hours each day keeping a few holes open to the surface. By the end of the winter, they have made a tunnel through the ice just wide enough for their body to pass through. There may be another meter (3 feet) of snow on top of the ice, but enough air gets to the seal below.

JOINING TOGETHER

The biggest structure in the world, the Great Barrier Reef, was built by tiny sea creatures about the size of a pinhead. It is called coral.

These animals have only a mouth, tentacles, and a stomach. The tentacles trap food and bring sea water into the coral's stomach. Lime from the sea water is used to build a skeleton around its soft body. When one coral animal dies, another builds on top of its skeleton. Over the years, as millions of tiny coral live and die, a coral reef grows. The reef becomes home to hundreds of species of animals.

Animals that can...

Have you ever swallowed a mouthful of saltwater? Yuck! Most plants and animals use either saltwater or freshwater. But many creatures have learned to use both types.

Sea gulls can drink saltwater. The salt is taken out of their bodies by a pair of salt glands. It then passes out through the gull's nostrils.

Sockeye salmon are born in freshwater, but move to the ocean to grow. They return to the streams where they were born when it's time to lay eggs. They look different though. In the ocean salmon are silvery blue. In freshwater they are bright red and olive green.

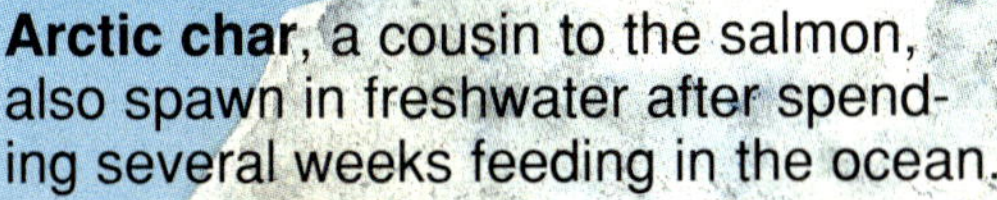

Arctic char, a cousin to the salmon, also spawn in freshwater after spending several weeks feeding in the ocean.

....CHANGE!

The seashore changes a lot as the tides go in and out. Each creature finds its own special place to live on the beach.

The saber-toothed blenny is a most unusual fish. It can leave the water and crawl from pool to pool using its fins.

In the area farthest from the water, where only the ocean spray or a very high tide will reach, live creatures like **periwinkle snails**[1] and **acorn barnacles**.[2]

Limpets,[3] **chitons**[4] and **crabs**[5] live closer to the water's edge and are covered by high tides.

Some seashore creatures live underwater except at low tide. They include **sea stars**,[6] **urchins**,[7] **mussels**[8] and **anemones**.[9]

Only the occasional very low tide leaves the **abalones**,[10] **sea cucumbers**[11] and **octopuses**[12] out of the water.

What's for Dinner?

The variety of life at the seashore provides plenty of food for the animals that live there.

Bloodworms live in pin-sized holes just below the high tide mark. These small red worms eat tiny animals that live in the sand. **Sandpipers**, in turn, eat bloodworms.

Yellow and black gobi are like little vacuum cleaners. They clean the skin of larger fish — sometimes they even clean the fish's mouth!

The **periwinkle snail** eats algae growing on plants and rocks. Its tiny tongue is covered with 3,500 teeth. Scraping this rough tongue over the surface helps the long process of turning rock to sand.

Beach hoppers are scavengers that help to clean the beach. They eat grass and kelp as well as dead fish and crabs. Beach hoppers can travel a long way during a day; they use the position of the moon to find their way home.

When they eat, **moon snails** wrap their large foot around a shellfish. Then they drill through the shell to eat the soft meat inside.

To eat an oyster, a **starfish** will grip it in a bear hug. When the oyster's muscles tire its shell opens. The starfish's stomach moves out of its body into the oyster. Once dinner is finished, the stomach moves back into the starfish.

The **giant clam** is one of the largest shellfish. Its shell can be almost a meter (3 feet) across and weigh up to 260 kg (about 600 pounds). Sea plants and animals grow on the shell. When it closes its shell, the clam eats the plants and animals trapped inside.

Can you find other animals we've talked about? Who's hunting what for dinner?

Hide Me

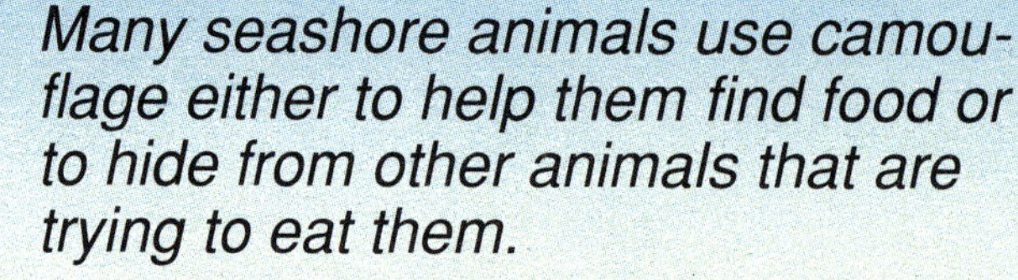

Many seashore animals use camouflage either to help them find food or to hide from other animals that are trying to eat them.

When sneaking up on prey, a **polar bear** covers its nose with a paw. How might this help the bear hide?

The octopus is a master of disguise. It can quickly change its color to match its surroundings. It can look just like a clump of seaweed or a rock or blend in with the open water.

Flounders have flat bodies. Both eyes are on one side of the adult's body. They are light on one side and dark on the other. Why do you think they swim on their side?

Spider or **decorator crabs** attach pieces of algae, sponge, jellyfish and wood chips to their bodies. This makes it difficult for other animals to find the crab.

Tidepool sculpins hide themselves in the sand with only their eyes showing. Their green, red, brown and black colors come from the small plants and animals they eat.

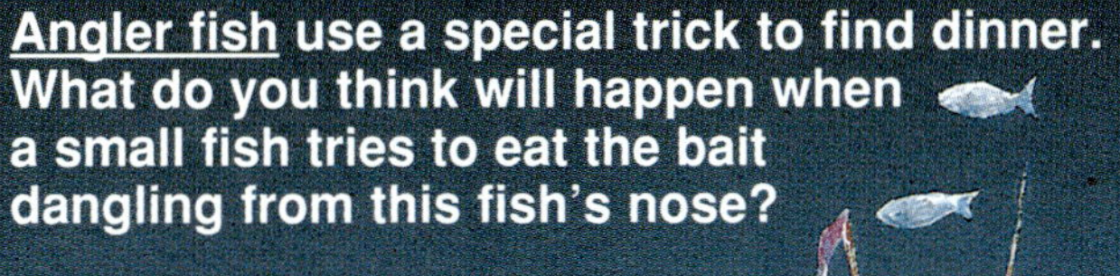

Angler fish use a special trick to find dinner. What do you think will happen when a small fish tries to eat the bait dangling from this fish's nose?

The female gall crab lets coral grow around her. A male can enter her little cave, and babies can leave. To eat she filters food from the water. She is trapped, but safe.

Empty shells make good homes for hermit crabs since they cannot make their own.

A World is Born

The seashore is the nursery of the sea. That's because so many animals are born along the water's edge.

Turtles travel up the beach when it is time to lay their eggs. The mother digs a hole and lays about one hundred eggs. Only a few will survive. When the eggs are hatched, the babies have to scramble out of the hole and cross the beach to the open sea.

At Turtle Islands National Park in Malaysia, turtles are protected.

It is easier to float in saltwater than freshwater. Saltwater is more buoyant. Try this experiment:

1. Place an uncooked egg in a glass of warm water.

2. Stir in salt until the egg begins to float.

This buoyancy provides a good home for fish eggs. They float near the surface of the water where the sunlight and oxygen help them to develop.

The female **blue mussel** can release up to twenty-five million eggs each time it reproduces. The young ride on ocean currents. Some grow into adult mussels. What happens to most of them?

A rocky ledge on a cliff is home for some sea birds. **Guillemot** eggs are a pointed oval shape so they will not roll off the edge.

STAY AWAY FROM MY BABIES!

Sea birds have several different ways of keeping their eggs safe. For example, some penguins, like the emperor penguin, do not need a nest. The egg will be kept warm on the father's feet, covered by a fold of skin.

Swallows and **swifts** build their nests out of mud on a cliff or steep rock wall.

Terns scrape out a shallow hole for their eggs above the high tide line and rely on camouflage to protect them.

SEASHORE

Life at the seashore holds many surprises for the careful observer.

The **pelican's** pouch is like a plate for its babies. Adult birds bring up partly digest-ed food. They hold it in their pouch for their babies to eat.

If a **starfish** loses an arm, it can grow another one.

A **seahorse** is the only fish that uses its tail to wrap around seaweed. The female lays her eggs in the father's belly. He looks after the eggs until they hatch.

If there aren't enough male fish, female **cleaner wrasses** can turn into males in order to fertilize eggs.

Swimming with their feet, **cormorants** can dive to a depth of about 30 meters or 100 feet.

The **coquina** is a very small, lav-ender-colored clam. It pulls itself under the sand with a pink foot that acts like an anchor. It feeds through tubes that filter food from the ocean water.

ODDITIES

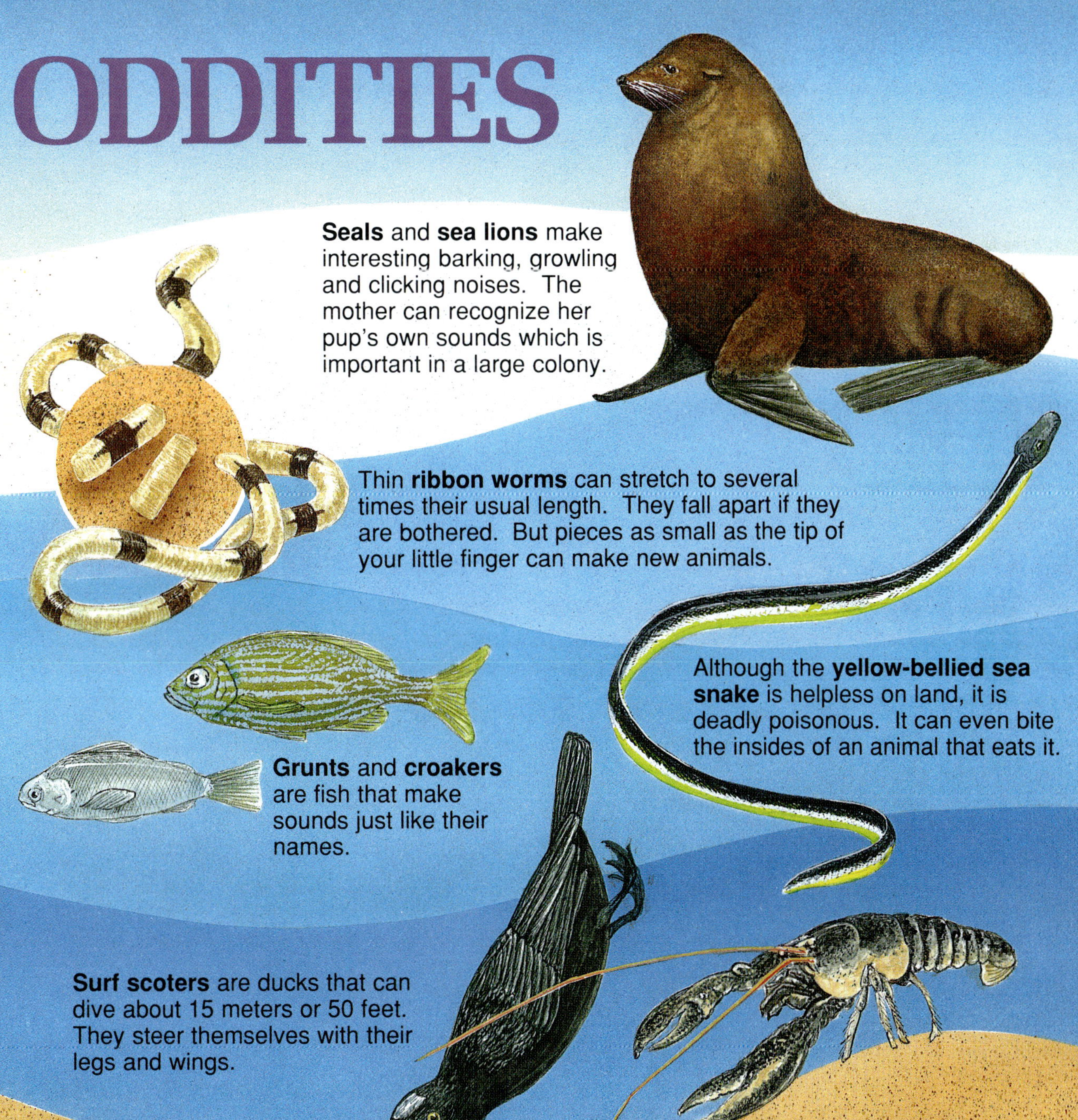

Seals and **sea lions** make interesting barking, growling and clicking noises. The mother can recognize her pup's own sounds which is important in a large colony.

Thin **ribbon worms** can stretch to several times their usual length. They fall apart if they are bothered. But pieces as small as the tip of your little finger can make new animals.

Although the **yellow-bellied sea snake** is helpless on land, it is deadly poisonous. It can even bite the insides of an animal that eats it.

Grunts and **croakers** are fish that make sounds just like their names.

Surf scoters are ducks that can dive about 15 meters or 50 feet. They steer themselves with their legs and wings.

The **lobster** has very weak eyes. It relies on tiny hairs covering its body to guide it.

Interesting Finds

There is a lot happening at any beach. To see it you must look carefully. How many holes do you see? Each of these holes is a doorway to some animal's home. Other animals live beneath dried seaweed and under debris left at the high tide line. How many animals can you find?

Kelp is the name for any large brown seaweed. You can guess what the weather will be like by touching kelp washed onto the beach. If the dried leaves feel sticky, it's going to rain. If they're dry and brittle, it will be nice.

MAKE A SHELL COLLECTION

There are four major types of sea shells:

1. Snails have univalve shells. "Uni" means one. **Univalve** shells are all in one piece.
2. Clams have **bivalve** shells. "Bi" means two. Bivalve shells have two halves with a hinge in the middle.
3. **Chiton** shells are made of eight overlapping pieces.
4. **Tusk** or **tooth** shells resemble an elephant's tusk.

How many types of shells can you find?

If you have collected some shells, keep them shiny by rubbing a little vegetable oil on them.

What shells whisper of the sea?

MAKE A SEA TREASURE BOX

Glue shells to the outside of a plastic container. What will you keep in your box?

MAKE A BEACH MAGNIFIER

A magnifier will help you find some seashore animals. You can make your own. Remove the labels from an empty glass jar. Fill it with water. Lay the jar on its side on the beach. What do you see?

PEOPLE and the Seashore

The seashore is filled with many different creatures and plants that depend on each other to live and grow. This is the part of the ocean that is the most full of life.

Think of the seashore as a boundary between sea, land and air. A change in one will be felt all over. Life at the seashore is in a delicate balance.

Sometimes we hear about an oil spill on the ocean. Oil has leaked from a huge tanker. Often it will wash up onto the shore, covering everything in a gooey mass. If the oil coats a bird's feathers, it cannot fly. A sea otter cannot keep warm. Important food sources for all creatures become poisoned. Life at the seashore is in danger.

Scientists are working hard to find new ways to clean up oil spills quickly.

How do you think we might prevent an oil spill?

Sea salt is collected by evaporating sea water in some areas of the world. In Mexico, however, this has destroyed nesting areas for the Caribbean flamingo.

Many salt marshes are being drained to make room for farms and houses. Coastlines are sometimes built out to create new land. Harbors are dredged to make them deeper for larger ships. What will happen to the creatures that used to live there?

Some people have suggested towing huge icebergs to big cities to supply fresh water. But we don't know yet how this would affect the polar regions or the ocean water and weather patterns near the city.

When a lot of people live near a seashore, the type of life you will find there changes. Warmer water in many city harbors hosts different life than in colder waters nearby. Often one species will do very well while all others die. Warmer water can cause some creatures, like shrimp, to mature faster.

Could the same super-strong "glue" used by barnacles be copied for our use?

Does the sea cucumber contain a miracle medicine?

Can the cleaner wrasse show us how to cure an infection without drugs?

There are many secrets that we have yet to learn from the sea.

There is much to learn about the seashore. Next time you are there look carefully. Be a good observer. Perhaps you can discover one of the ocean's secrets.

We would like to thank the Ontario Arts Council
for their assistance in the production of this book.